Beginner's Pocket Guide to

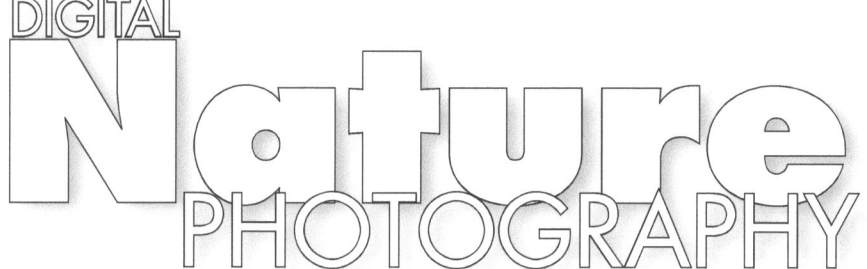

DIGITAL Nature PHOTOGRAPHY

by Kevin C. Loughlin

Beginner's Pocket Guide to Digital Nature Photography

Published by
Wildside Nature Tours
241 Emerald Drive
Yardley, PA 19067
www.WildsideNatureTours.com

Copyright © 2012 by Wildside Nature Tours, Yardley, Pennsylvania

ISBN-13: 978-0984945801

ISBN-10: 0984945806

For general information on our other products, tours, workshops and services, please contact us within the USA at 888.875.9453 and outside the USA at 610.564.0941.

All photos © Kevin C. Loughlin and Wildside Nature Tours
Photos of Kevin were taken by Paula Mandracchia

DIGITAL Nature PHOTOGRAPHY is

98% PATIENCE
1% LUCK
1% SKILL

- Learn your equipment
- Learn your subject
- Be ready
- Be quick
...and *Be Low Impact!*

Do not disturb the wildlife you are trying to photograph...
Their well being is more important than your image!

Take only photographs, Leave only footprints...

Beginner's Pocket Guide to
Digital Nature Photography

Booklet Description

So many books try to cover every possible tidbit of information, which can often become overwhelming to the beginner. This booklet, however, will cover the absolute basics of nature photography using a digital camera. The use of shutter speed and aperture for proper exposure control will be discussed as well as determining the best composition. We will examine the settings and capabilities of digital cameras in general, not one specific camera.

This booklet will not replace your instruction book for how to use your specific camera, the instruction book that came with your camera is intended for that purpose. Please thoroughly read your instruction book in order to have an understanding of the features of your camera. This booklet will then teach you how and when to apply the **useful** features your camera has.

Once you have learned the basic rules well, you will have a better understanding of when and how to break these rules and take some artistic license as you grow and expand your skills, equipment and explorations!

About the Author

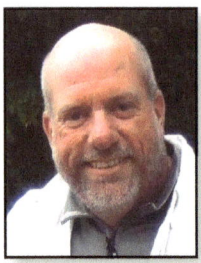

Kevin Loughlin was raised to appreciate nature while exploring the woodlands and streams of Pennsylvania as a child. At age six, during a family trip through the American West, Kevin became fascinated with photography as well seeing the new and different birds throughout North America. Instilled with a love for travel and exploring new, exciting destinations he felt a desire to share his experiences with others and in 1993 Wildside Nature Tours was founded.

Kevin's photographs and articles have appeared in publications such as WildBird, Audubon and Philadelphia Magazines, as well as many natural history books and websites, including National Geographic and World Wildlife sites.

Kevin teaches photography and birding courses through several adult education venues as well as through seminars and workshops for groups, organizations and schools. Currently the vice president of the Birding Club of Delaware County, Kevin also founded the PA Young Birder's Club, sharing his love of nature while inspiring kids to get outside.

Camera types

Ultra Compact

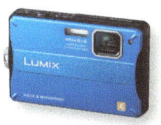

These tiny cameras are great for family events and for those who prefer to travel light. They are small enough to fit into a shirt pocket, yet offer the resolution (not to be confused with quality) of the larger cameras. With new lens technologies available, there is also no apparent loss in image quality in a **4x6 print** for these miniatures. The only drawbacks are the additional cost for miniaturization, minimal zoom capabilities and "noisier" images due to the smaller image sensor size.

Compact

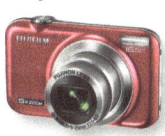

More traditional in size for a point-and-shoot camera, most compacts are a little too big to fit into a shirt pocket, though most will still fit into pockets of baggy pants or a small purse. Most of these models have 4x zooms, though some may be even more powerful. This type of camera will be the most economical to purchase.

ZLR (Zoom Lens Reflex)

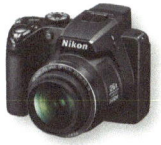

A Zoom Lens Reflex camera will offer more of the feel (and size) of a small DSLR type camera, but with a built-in zoom lens rather than true interchangeable lenses. The zooms are much stronger than the smaller models—which makes sense—current can be 20x optical zoom or more. Some models even offer image stabilizers for their high magnification. Many ZLRs have the ability to add filters or accessory lenses for more versatility. Some allow the use of an add-on, more powerful flash as well.

DSLR (Digital Single Lens Reflex)

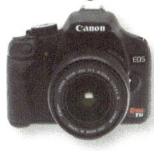

Single Lens Reflex cameras offer the advantage of being able to remove the lens and replace it with another of different magnification. The ability to add wide angle or super telephoto lenses is the biggest appeal of these models. Many other accessories may be used as well, such as filters or more powerful flashes.

The DLSR advantage:
- Larger sensor dimensions (not to be confused with megapixels) for better quality.
- Brighter, truer image view - you look directly through the lens, not into a mini-EVF.
- Interchangeable lenses for versatility from utra-wide angle to big, bright telephoto.
- More control over shutter speed and aperture with much wider range of settings.
- No "shutter lag" like the compact cameras have when the shutter release is pressed.

Basic Glossary of Digital Terms

Instruction Book

An analog, informational instrument with often confusing terms and definitions, usually translated from Japanese into very poor English.

Pixel / Megapixel

The tiny dots that make up an image, like a mosaic, are the pixels. One million pixels equals one megapixel, the measurement used to describe a camera sensor's resolution. This measurement will determine the final "sharpness" of an enlargement. (i.e. Six megapixels will make a maximum 20x30 print of good quality.)

Resolution

Image quality, only as measured by the number of pixels in a given amount of image space. Higher resolution equals higher quality of image and larger printable size. However, a larger image sensor will offer better overall quality (see below).

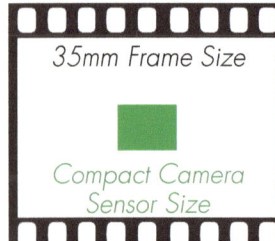

Compared to 35mm film, the image at left shows the size of a typical compact camera image sensor. The image on the right shows a typical DSLR image sensor (APS-C)—most pro model DSLRs now offer full 35mm frame sensors sizes.

The larger size allows the image sensor to capture a wider range of color and contrast information with the least amount of data loss (noise) in the image.

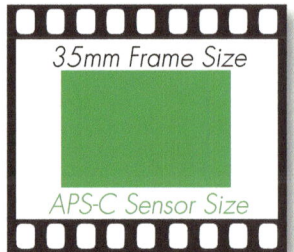

JPEG Compression

The means by which a digital photo is "packed smaller" to conserve data storage space. JPEG (.jpg) is the current standard compression scheme used by camera manufacturers. The higher the compression ratio, however, the lower quality the image will be as image information (pixels) will be discarded or "lost."

RAW (NEF)

A lossless image file type which allows more post processing capabilities. Images created in RAW (or Nikon's NEF) format are most similar to film when using filters, however, they also need the most image processing before printing or other uses.

ISO

An adjustable number that indicates the light sensitivity of the camera's sensor. A lower number is less sensitive and requires more light. Higher number requires less light, however, may also cause more image artifacts, known as "noise".

Noise

Noise appears as mis-colored pixels, image "glitches," or as a "grainy" texture to the image and is most noticeable in photos taken in low light or set to a high ISO. It is caused by pixels that were not stimulated by light, it is usually due to poor sensor quality or small sensor size. Noise will vary greatly between camera models.

Shutter Lag (non-DSLR cameras)

The amount of time between pressing the shutter release to when the shutter actually fires is called shutter lag. Every model of camera will be different, for different reasons. There are several variables that make up this lag time, some of which can be compensated for by practicing some basic tips.

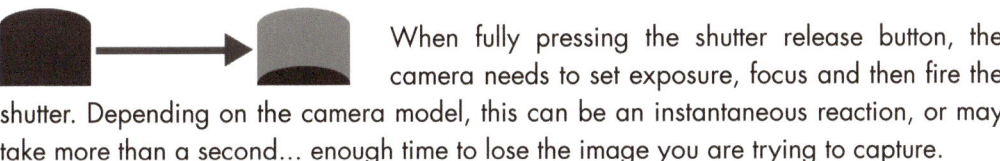

When fully pressing the shutter release button, the camera needs to set exposure, focus and then fire the shutter. Depending on the camera model, this can be an instantaneous reaction, or may take more than a second... enough time to lose the image you are trying to capture.

By pre-focusing on your subject, you can reduce your total lag time. Point the camera at your subject, press the button half way to force the camera to focus and set exposure, then wait for the decisive moment to take the picture. Adjusting for the actual lag time of your camera.

Learn how long the actual lag time of your camera model is by pre-focusing, then pressing the shutter the rest of the way. A typical compact camera will still have a momentary delay which you will need to compensate for by pressing the release just before the decisive moment. (Remember: DSLR cameras have no lag time with which to contend.)

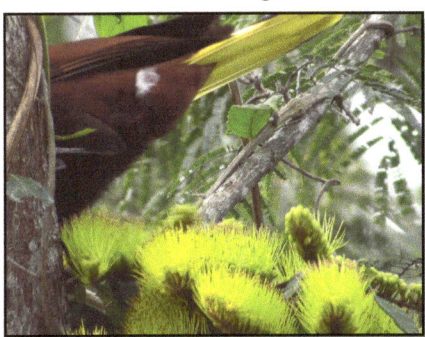

Shutter lag was not compensated for in the above image... leaving us with the departing view of an otherwise beautiful subject.

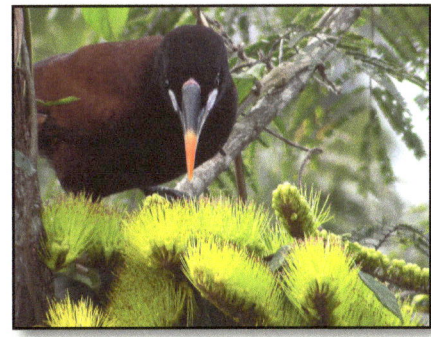

By pre-focusing the camera and waiting for the decisive moment, a much more desirable image was produced of the Montezuma's Oropendola.

White Balance

Color Temperature

The color of light is measured on the Kelvin scale. Full sunlight measures about 5600°-6000°— a very "blue" light on the Kelvin scale. Tungsten or incandescent light measures about 3200°—very orange. This is why when photographing with film in living room light the colors never look right. Most film is balanced for daylight, and to correct for artificial light one must use filters. However, digital cameras have filters built in to correct for many different lighting conditions. These filters are controlled using the White Balance menu on your camera.

AWB (Auto White Balance)

The Auto White Balance setting of a digital camera measures the color balance of the available light and adjusts the internal 'filter' accordingly. Though the AWB usually works well, as with most automatic systems it is not perfect. There is often a color hue remaining that detracts from the final image. This hue can sometimes be corrected in photo editing software, but it is usually best to correct it in the camera by using one of the manual settings. (Note: RAW/NEF images can be adjusted later in your RAW conversion software, however, JPEG files have less adjustability.)

Sunlight / Daylight Setting

Daylight is very blue. Other colors in a scene, however, can throw off the AWB of a camera, causing the colors to be less vivid or just "not quite right." By setting the white balance to the SUN setting colors will be more accurate.

Cloudy / Shade Setting

On cloudy days or in the shade, the AWB may cause colors to appear "cold" with a bluish tint. Setting the camera to the proper mode will "warm-up" the scene to create a more vivid image.

Incandescent Setting

Living room lamps and stage lighting will create an orange cast in an image, even with AWB. However, by setting the mode to the LIGHTBULB (incandescent) setting, a more natural color will be recorded. It may not be perfect, however, as different wattage bulbs may be different color temperatures.

AWB vs. Manual White Balance

The Auto White Balance setting is practical for most situations outside, however, it is not always perfect. Scenes which have a majority of one color, such as these ferns, may require a manual white balance setting in order to achieve the desired natural color. This setting is much more important when shooting JPEG images than RAW files, as RAW processing software has manual white balance settings.

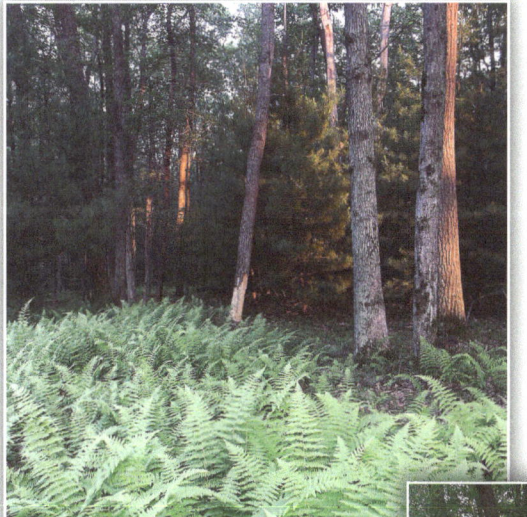

AWB used on these ferns during a setting sun created a bluish color cast, taking away from the true quality of the evening glow. The image is flat and lifeless.

Manually setting the white balance to the "direct sun" setting removed all of the bluish cast and allowed for the correct color of the sunset to make the scene glow.

Exposure Basics

Auto vs. Manual Exposure

Apertures and shutter speeds work together for correct exposure. A faster speed requires a larger aperture (and vise versa) to allow the proper amount of light to hit the sensor. Automatic exposure systems in most cameras try to strike a happy medium, allowing for a fast enough shutter speed to hand hold the camera. This usually works well, however, it is not always perfect in every situation.

Many cameras have some manual exposure capabilities that allow the user to set shutter speed or aperture or both. Even within the auto exposure modes of most cameras, users are able to prioritize a higher speed or smaller aperture depending on the subject and desired effect.

Shutter Speed

Measured in fractions of a second (or full seconds for time exposures), shutter speeds determine the amount of time light is allowed to hit the image sensor. Faster shutter speeds allow for stopping action. Slow shutter speeds require a tripod to eliminate camera shake. Most compact digital cameras allow some control of shutter speeds though they may have a limited range of speeds. A typical DSLR will range from 30 seconds to 1/4000 of a second or even faster, whereas a compact camera will have a smaller range from about 1 second to 1/1000.

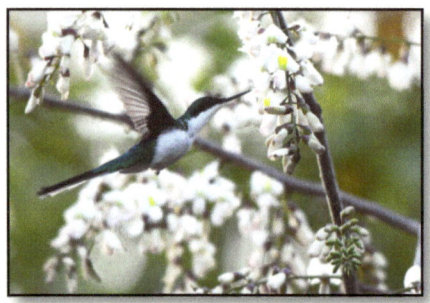

1/500 of a second allowed for a nearly stop-action shot of this hummingbird.

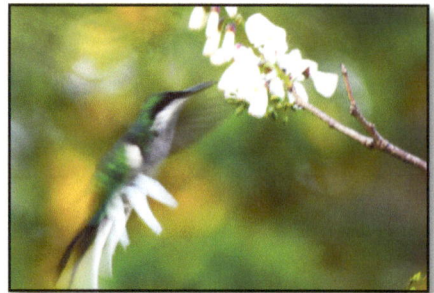

1/60 of a second created an artistic blur of the same hummingbird.

Aperture

The lens aperture allows variable amounts of light to enter the camera to expose the sensor to light. Measured in "f" numbers, the largest apertures have the smallest f number. Smaller apertures, a larger number. Most compact digital cameras have a very limited aperture range, usually f/2.8—f/8. Apertures on DSLR camera lenses can be as large as f/1.4 to as small as f/32. The aperture not only controls the amount of light to hit the image sensor, it also controls "depth-of-field" or the area of focus in front of and behind your point of

Depth-of-Field

Depth-of-field is the area of an image that is in focus. Always 1/3 in front of and two thirds behind your focus point will be in focus. Depending upon the aperture used, the actual distance will vary. A large aperture may only allow 1" in front and 2" behind your focus point actually, in focus where as a small aperture may be 10' in front and 20' behind. The use of a small aperture or large aperture to control depth will depend on the subject and how you want it to be presented. Experiment!

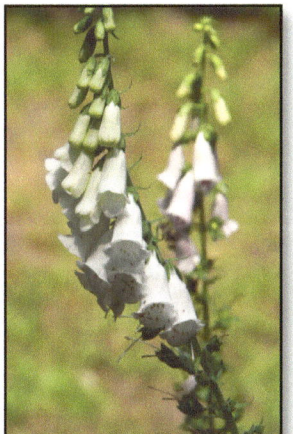

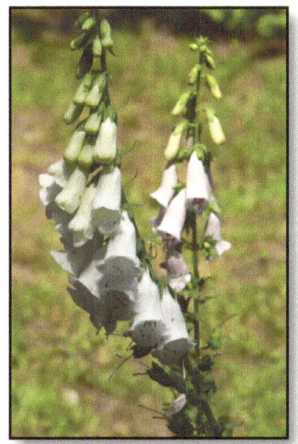

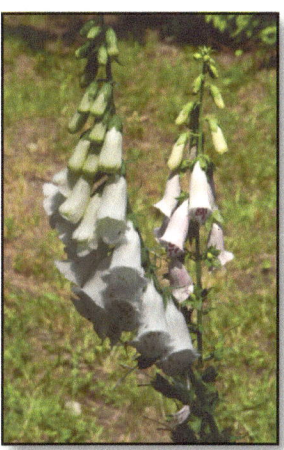

Aperture f/8, the smallest available in most compact cameras. Background pleasantly blurred.

Aperture f/16, available on all SLR lenses, creates a slightly distracting background in this image.

Aperture f/32, available on some DSLR lenses, in this instance creates a very distracting background.

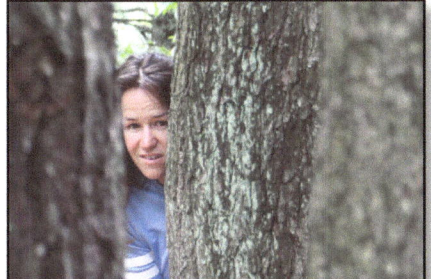

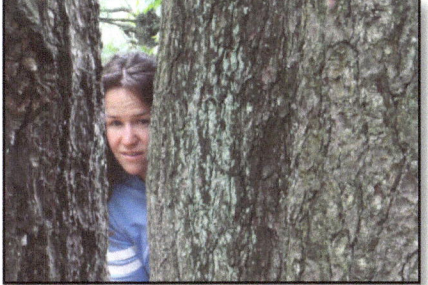

At an aperture of f/5.6, focusing on the subject's eyes created a blurred background and foreground forcing the viewer to concentrate on the subject.

At an aperture of f/32, everything is in focus. The subject is lost within the image and the viewer is distracted.

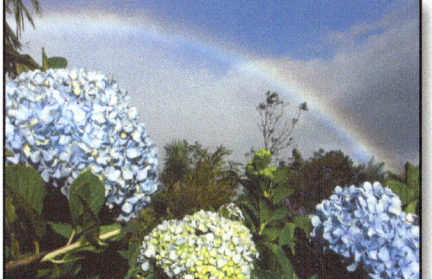

Everything from near to far in this image is in focus, which in this case is what makes the image. At f/32, the flowers close-up and the rainbow in the distance are all leading the eye around.

Composition

Balance the Elements

On one level or another, everyone responds better to a picture that has all elements in balance. Lead the eye along an interesting path through the photo, with the use of strong lines or patterns. Keep the horizon level. Crop out extra elements that you are not interested in. Place your subject where you think it most belongs rather than just accepting it wherever it happens to land in the photo. Play with perspective so that all lines show a pattern or lead the eye to your main subject.

Rule of thirds

By splitting your view into thirds, both vertically and horizontally, you are able to better position your subject for a more pleasing image.

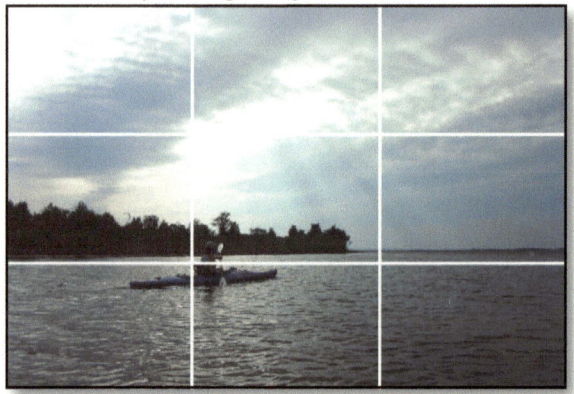

Your main "point of interest" should be placed at one of the four intersecting points on the grid. Your horizon should be placed along one of the horizontal lines. If your subjects are moving, try to place them so they are moving into the image. Motionless wildlife should be looking into the frame... close-ups should place the eyes at one of the points of interest.

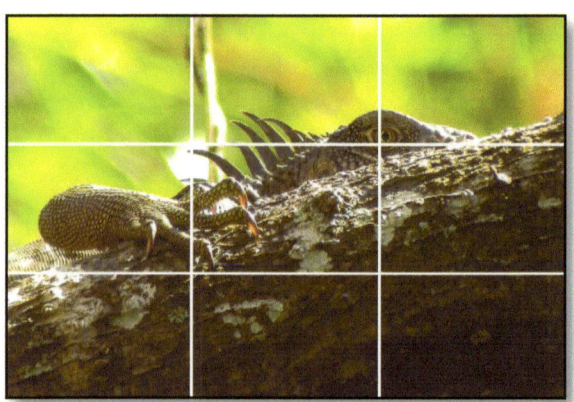

Composition (continued)

Be Conscious of Your Background

The proper background can make or break an image. Beware of distracting elements or poor lighting conditions and change you angle to improve the image to make your subject stand out. One way to do this is to move closer to your subject (time and subject wariness allowing). Each time you spot a subject, snap a shot and then move in closer for a better shot. Having your subject almost fill the frame helps your viewer understand and appreciate your photo. Also, details are often more interesting than an overall view. Keep moving in (or zooming) closer until you are sure the photo will successfully represent your subject.

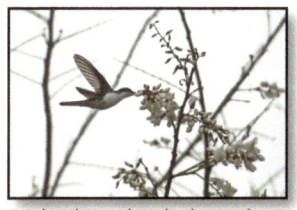

Good subject, but background too bright with distracting branches.

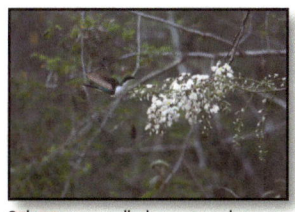

Subject too small, distracting elements in background.

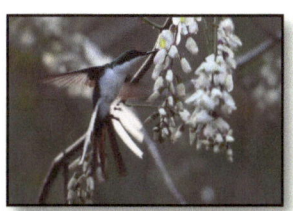

Background not distracting, subject fills frame, good composition.

Discern what interests you and center your efforts on getting the best photo of that subject whether it's a landscape, an animal, a flower, a mood or a culture. Then be sure to keep anything that would distract out of the picture. The easiest way to do this is to watch your borders—the edges of the image you see through the camera's viewfinder. Then recompose if anything—such as an unattractive telephone wire or branch, an old soda can or a distracting sign—hangs into your picture.

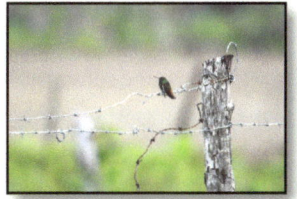

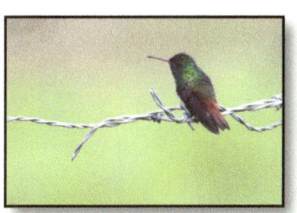

Top image too far away, with distracting elements. Slowly, safely stalking subject allowed for a better image with no distractions.

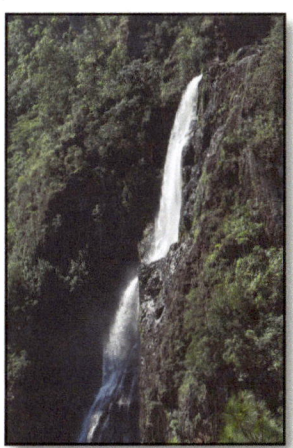

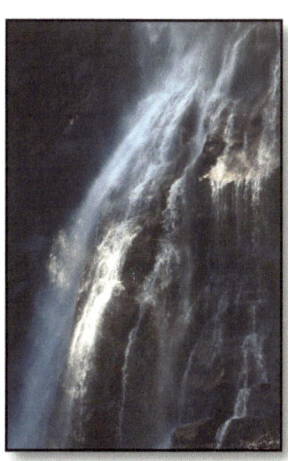

Image on left is a typical snapshot of a waterfall, showing the whole subject. By zooming in on the most interesting elements of the subject, a much more pleasing final image can be obtained. Take your time and concentrate on what is most appealing about your subject, then concentrate on that.

Advanced Exposure Control

Exposure Compensation

Auto exposure is not perfect, and may be fooled in high contrast or low contrast situations. Most cameras have the ability to compensate for these odd lighting situations without using a fully manual mode. Usually denoted by a +/- symbol, a variation of up to two f-stops can often be made. A basic rule for exposure compensation is +1-stop for a dark subject with a bright background, -1-stop for a bright subject against a dark background. All situations will be slightly different so experiment every chance you get so will be ready for any situation.

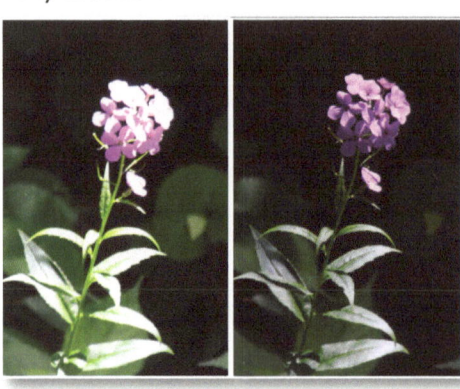 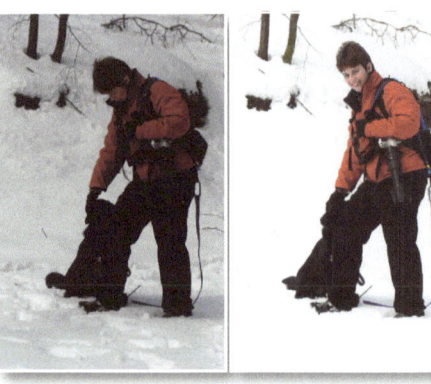

A dark background with a lit subject requires less exposure. The left image was with the Auto setting, the image on the right was with a -2.0 exposure compensation.

A bright background requires more exposure. The left image was with the Auto setting, the image on the right was with a +1.0 exposure compensation.

Timed Exposures

Night or low-light photography is tricky. Digital cameras are great for this in that you can experiment to your heart's content with no additional cost. They are bad for night photography because of the "noise" factor previously discussed. Long exposures in low light will often create a noisy image. Remember to always use a tripod for long exposures!

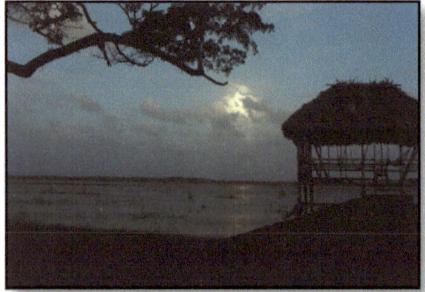 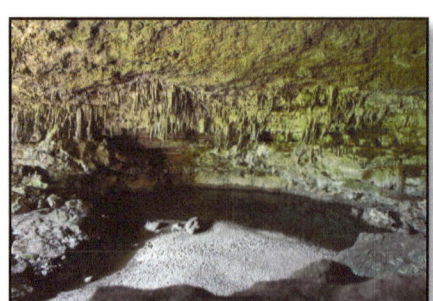

This image of a moonrise over a lake only needed a 1/2 second exposure. A tripod was used to steady the camera for the long exposure in the mild breeze.

This image of the inside of a cave near the entrance required a 2 second exposure. A rock was used to steady the camera for this exposure.

Shutter Speeds

Control the Speed for Effect

Proper use of shutter speeds can make or break and image. Most cameras, even compacts have the ability to control shutter speeds. For some reason, most people always want to stop the action. In some cases this is great, however, in many cases a stop action image is too static, with no sense of what is actually happening. The blur of a running animal offers the excitement of the chase. Panning with your subject highlights the subject and separates them from the background.

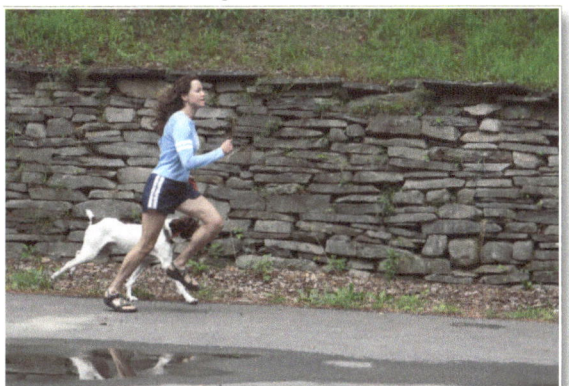

A note on shutter speeds and lenses: The basic rule of thumb to eliminate camera shake—use a shutter speed equal to or greater than the 35mm equivalent focal length of the lens you are using. (200mm=1/200 sec.)

STOP ACTION
1/1000 gives a sharp stop action with the dog appearing as he is airborne. This is great for showing subject detail in movement.

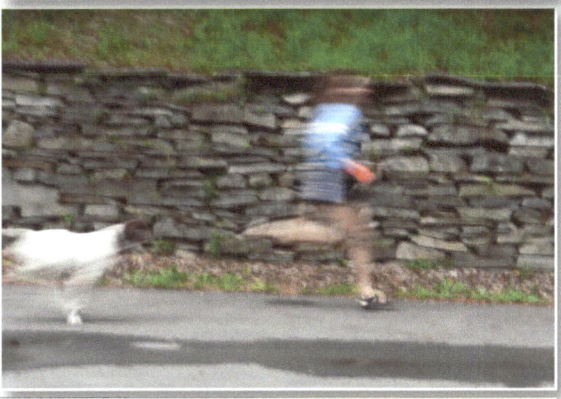

MOTION BLUR
1/15 while holding the camera still show the subject in motion, albeit unrecognizably. This can be used in an artistic way with many subjects.

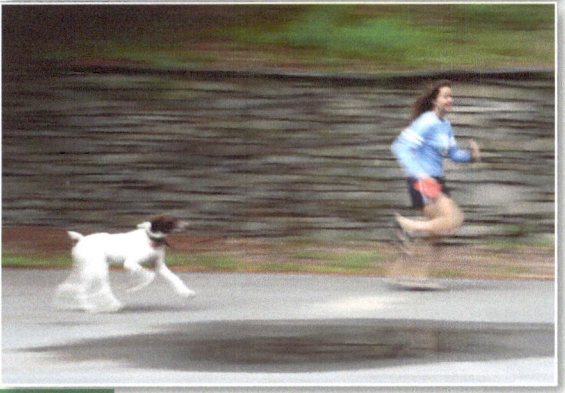

PANNING
1/15 while following the subject—after releasing the shutter, continue to follow the subject—creates a true feeling of movement while keeping the subject much more recognizable.

Shutter Speeds

Power or Tranquility

Changing shutter speeds can help create different moods.

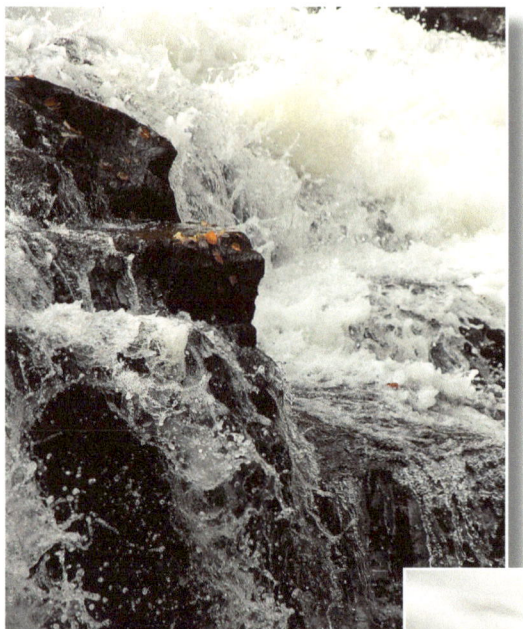

STOP ACTION
A fast shutter speed of 1/1000 stopped the waterfall to show each droplet creating a feeling of power.

THE VEIL EFFECT
A shutter speed of 1 second or longer creates a veil effect, portraying the tumbling water soft image that offers a feeling of tranquility.

Filters

Protect Your Investment with an UV Filter

A UV (Ultra-Violet) filter will offer a protective shield on the front of your lenses. These clear filters are not meant to change the image, but only protect your lens from getting damaged. Be sure to get a good quality filter as cheap filters may lower the quality significantly.

Reduce Reflections with a Polarizing Filter

A Circular Polarizing Filter or C-PL Filter is designed to reduce or eliminate reflections from any non-metallic surface. The "Circular" in the name does not refer to the shape of the filter but rather the direction in which the polarized coatings are applied to the lenses. All modern cameras require the use of this circular coating to function properly. A "Linear Polarizer" will not allow modern cameras to focus properly.

Rotating the polarizing filter 1/4 turn may change the image drastically, depending on the angle to the sun. Facing north or south will offer more of a change the facing east or west. This "effect" can be used to see into water, to get deeper blue skies or to help saturate the colors of fall foliage or springtime flowers.

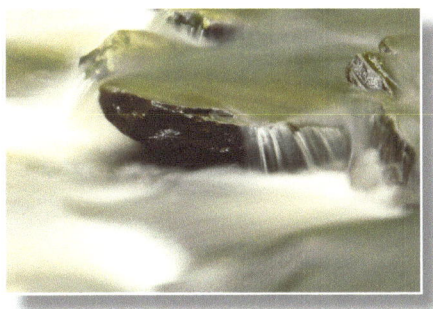

The above and below images are NOT Polarized.

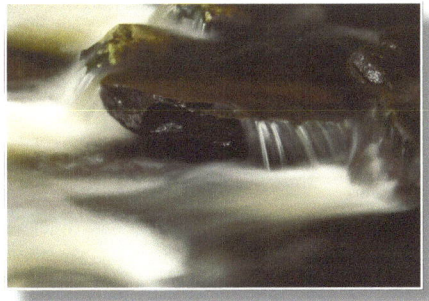

The above and below images ARE Polarized.

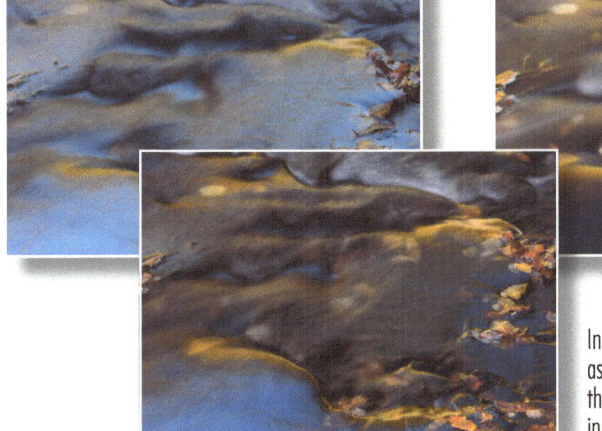

In order to keep some of the blue sky reflection as well as get more color in the autumn leaves, the polarizing filter was rotated only 1/8 turn in the image at left.

Using Flash

Flash as Main Light Source

For most snapshooters, use of the flash is limited to dark scenes where the flash is the main or only light source. Limited to the output of the flash, the distance a photo may be taken us usually minimal. Most compact camera flashes reach no more than 15 feet. Some DSLR accessory flashes, however, will reach 50 or 60 feet. Remember, though, that the flash cannot properly expose two subjects at different distances within the same scene. Because of this, foreground objects can be washed out, while backgrounds will be dark. Choose subject location wisely! An advantage of flash in low light is that it will stop action if used as a main light source.

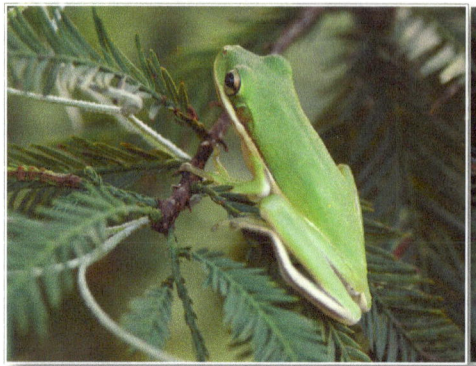

Green Tree Frog photographed in late evening sun.

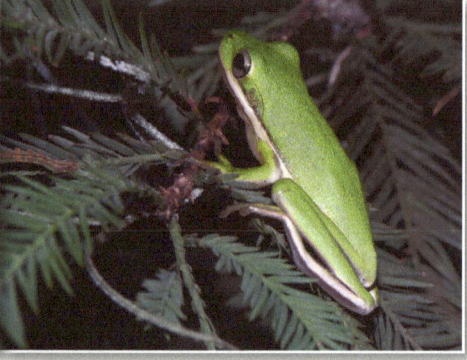

Green Tree Frog photographed with flash as main light.

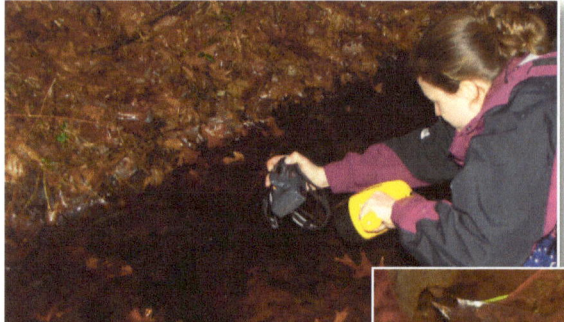

A flash is a necessity for photographing wildlife only seen at night. Here a spotlight is being used to light the subject well enough for the camera to focus. Be careful, if the light is too bright it will affect the quality of the image, too dim, the camera won't focus.

In this case we were photographing Spotted Salamanders in a few inches of water. Shooting at an angle to the water eliminated the chance of reflections.

Using Flash

Flash as Fill Light

Most people never think to turn their flash on outside on a sunny day. Of course not, why would it be necessary? In reality, a flash used on a sunny day can enhance your image by reducing unwanted shadows. Most cameras have a setting for fill-flash which forces the flash to fire all the time. Scrutinize your subjects, if there are unwanted shadows, use flash. If your subject is silhouetted against a bright background, using flash will expose for your subject while allowing the background to also be exposed properly. A flash used on a cloudy day or in deep shadow will enhance color on close-up subjects. A fill flash setting used in low light will produce some interesting effects by stopping some of the motion while the camera's shutter allows for a blurred effect on the rest of the image. Experiment, you may be pleasantly surprised with your results!

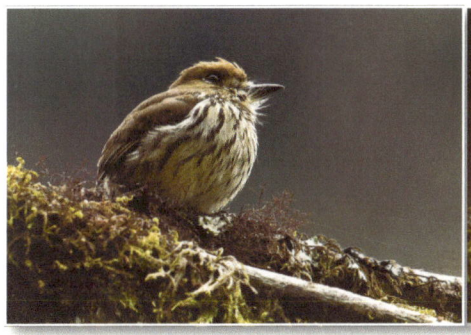

Although a good shot, with no flash, this Lanceolated Monklet appears dull in the shadows of early morning.

With a fill flash, the texture of the feathers come out, colors pop and the highlight in the eye adds more life.

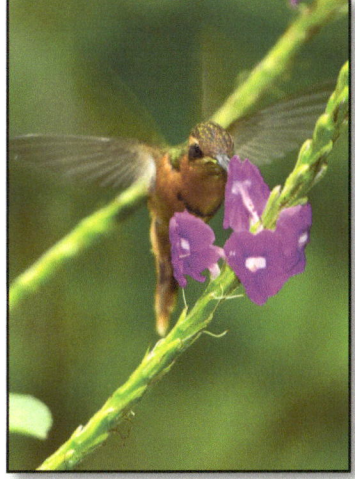

Experiment with slow shutter speeds and flash... you may be pleasantly surprised!

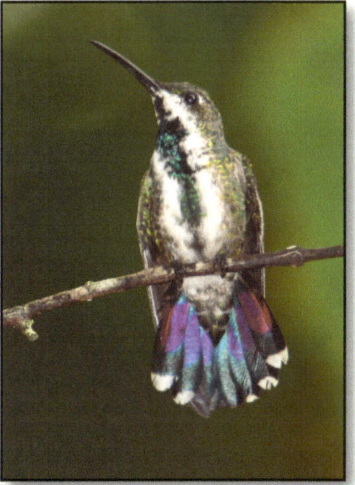

The flash brought out the brilliant color of this Green-breasted Mango hummingbird on a rather overcast day.

Your Camera's Lens

Lens Magnification

All cameras have a lens, that is how the light is focused onto the image sensor to create your photograph. However, not all lenses are created equal! Lens quality is important, as is determining the best focal length (magnification) for the scene. Non-DSLR digital cameras have a built-in zoom lens that varies the magnification of your photograph. Be sure only to compare optical zooms, not digital zooms! Digital zooms only enlarge the pixels in your image, destroying the image quality. *NOTE: Turn off the digital zoom in your camera!*

Non-DSLR digital lenses are rated as a magnification factor (e.g. 4x), however, this factor is not to be confused with actual magnification of the lens. It is actually a ratio of the lowest magnification or focal length to the highest. A compact digital that has a 7mm minimum focal length and a 21mm maximum focal length will be called a 3x zoom. However, the true magnification is really only 2.5x what your eye sees! Confused? Let's clear this up.

Since digital camera sensors are not all the same size, it is difficult to compare one camera to another—you need to know the image sensor size for each camera. However, since 35mm film cameras have been a standard for so long, the industry still uses these focal length numbers as the basis for comparison. For example, a 50mm lens on a 35mm film camera is a true 1x—it sees the same magnification as the human eye. This would mean that a 200mm lens would be a true 4x magnification. However, a compact digital camera may have a minimum focal length of 6mm, which depending on the image sensor size, may be the same magnification as a 36mm lens on a 35mm camera—which is slightly wider angle than what your eye sees, about a 0.7x magnification. Still confused?

Most digital camera manufacturers will give you the 35mm camera lens equivalents for comparison. For example, one camera model that touts a 10x lens is equivalent to a 38-380mm. Which means that the true maximum magnification is really only 7.6x. Another camera has a 12x with a maximum focal length of 420mm... true magnification 8.4x.

DSLR cameras offer interchangeable lenses. Most of the current models have an APS-C size image sensor, which has a 1.5x magnification factor over the 35mm focal length. This means a 50mm lens on a DSLR will be equivalent to a 75mm. A 400mm equivalent becomes a 600mm. This is great news for wildlife photographers looking to photograph hard to get close to subjects such as birds or bears. However, landscape photographers will have greater expense to get wide angle lenses. An 18mm wide angle lens was popular for 35mm film landscape photographers. However, in order to get an equivalent angle of view on a digital, a 12mm lens is needed... which are more difficult to come by and more expensive... and they must be made specifically for APS-C sensors!

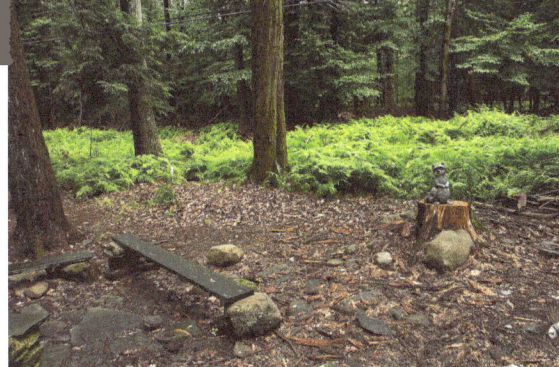

Focal Length Comparison

All images were taken from the same distance with a DSLR with an APS-C sensor. Focal lengths are listed in digital APS-C and full frame sensor designations.

18mm (27mm)

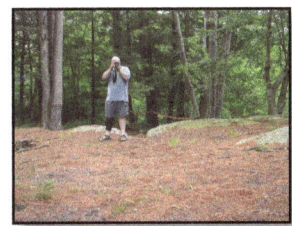

Subject's view of photographer showing distance from subject. (Same for all images at left.)

36mm (54mm)

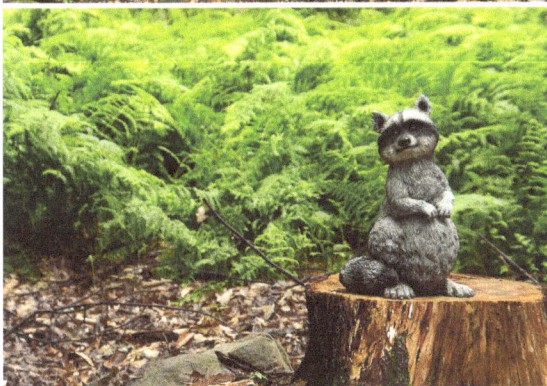

90mm (135mm)

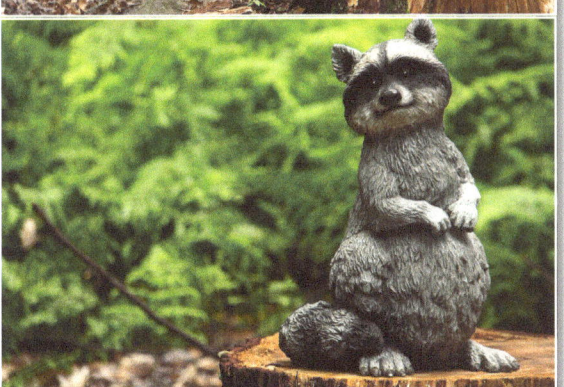

NOTE: Beware of unwanted background items sticking out of your subjects head!

200mm (300mm)

Lenses (continued)

Wide Angle

Since a 50mm lens on a 35mm film camera offers the same "magnification" as the human eye, a 35mm lens on a DSLR with a 1.5x magnification factor would be considered "normal." Therefore, any focal length smaller than 35mm would be a wide angle lens—see more in the frame than the normal lens.

Wide angle lenses are great for scenery as they allow you to view more in the image without moving further back. The smaller the focal length, the wider the angle of view. Currently, due to their small sensor size, few compact digital cameras have a wider lens than the film equivalent of 36mm. Those few compacts that do are only equal to about 28mm. Anything wider is very difficult to manufacture, and therefore cost prohibitive.

However, DSLR lenses are now available in focal lengths as small as 10mm (remember the 1.5x factor for the equivalent to a 15mm lens in a film camera). These lenses are fantastic for amazing landscape images if used correctly.

The most important compositional factor to remember with a wide angle lens is to have an "anchor" in the image to create a sense of depth in your photo—a flower, a rock or a tree in the foreground... anything that draws the eye into the image.

Telephoto

For a wildlife photographer, the magnification factor of a standard DSLR is great! A 400mm lens from a 35mm camera is now equal to a 600mm lens, perfect for birds and bears. The compact cameras also have a telephoto advantage. Some current ZLR models have an equivalent of a 500mm lens! However, they do this by using a much smaller sensor size... which equals lower quality images than a DSLR.

Zoom

Many people incorrectly use the term zoom to describe a telephoto lens. They are not one in the same. A zoom lens is a variable focal length lens—whether it be a telephoto zoom, a wide angle zoom or a wide angle to telephoto zoom. This is why, as discussed earlier, when a camera manufacturer says they have a 10x zoom, it is not an actual 10x magnification, but rather a ratio of smallest focal length to highest focal length.

Digital Zoom

Digital zoom is a term that should never be mentioned from the point you read this. Never use the digital zoom feature of your camera, it will only lower the image quality as it enlarges the pixels in your image. Turn it off and use only the optical zoom!

Perspective

Different focal length lenses will have different effects on you image's perspective.

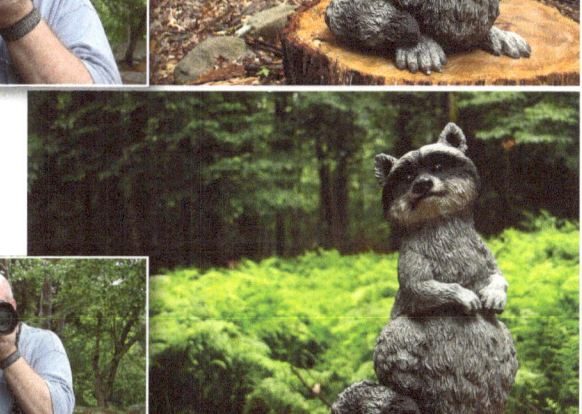

At 18mm (27mm) the photographer is close to the subject, background appears distant, apparent wide depth-of-field.

This perspective change is called telephoto compression. It causes the background to appear closer to the subject than it really is.

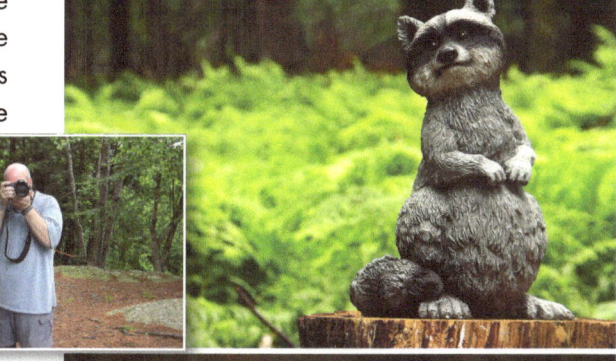

At 36mm (54mm) the photographer is less close to the subject, yet background appears closer, but less in focus.

In this series of images, the subject remains the same size while the photographer moves back and zooms in. However, the

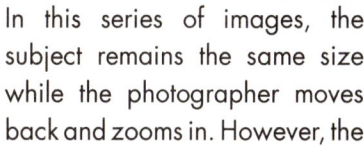

At 90mm (135mm) the photographer is further from the subject, yet the background appears closer and even less in focus.

background appears closer the further back the photographer moves. This effect can be used to create compelling images.

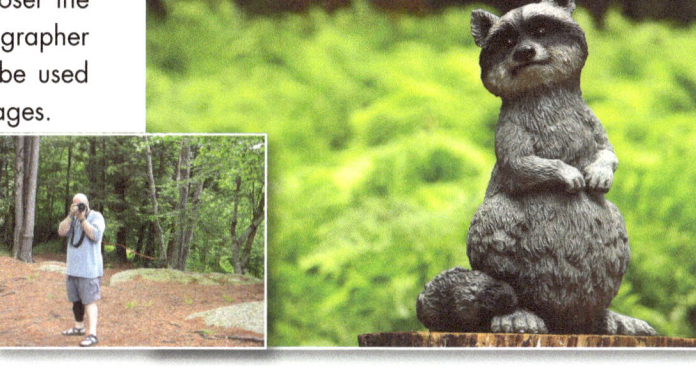

200mm (300mm) creates a closer and softer background, helping to separate the subject from the background.

Macro (Close-up) Photography

Macro Setting

All compact digital cameras have a macro or close-up setting usually indicated with a "flower" icon. Every camera's capabilities will be different, however, many digital cameras can focus within inches of the subject using this setting. Be careful to not fall into the trap of "if I am closer to my subject, I will get a closer picture." Using macro at the wide angle focal length you will be able to focus closer, however, by moving further back from your subject and zooming to telephoto (still in the macro mode), you will get more magnification of your subject, making it appear even closer.

Macro With a Magnifying Glass

A neat little trick to get even more magnification with your compact digital camera is to use a good quality magnifying glass in front of your lens. This will take some experimentation, and will not work well with every camera, but it is well worth the effort to try!

Macro Lens

The DSLR advantage prevails once again in the macro world. Most zoom lenses available for SLRs have a macro or close focus capability. Macro specific lenses are available also, allowing the photographer to get the greatest subject magnification and image quality. Typical macro lenses come in various fixed focal lengths of about 50mm, 100mm and 200mm (actual focal lengths will depend upon the manufacturer).

Extension Tubes

An extension tube, for DSLR cameras only, fits between the camera body and the lens. It is a tube—there is no glass in it. However, by adding the airspace behind the lens it changes the focus range of the lens (it will no longer focus to infinity). Available in different lengths—usually about 12mm, 25mm and 36mm—they can be used in any combination to allow the lens to move closer to the subject. The longer the length, the closer the lens can focus. This is an inexpensive way to get into real macro photography.

Close-up Filters

Similar to using a magnifying glass, close-up filters screw into the front of a DSLR's lens. They usually come in sets that include a +1, +2 and +4 and can be used in any combination to vary the magnification. Not the quality of a real macro lens nor extension tubes, they are relatively inexpensive for what they do!

Experiment with Macro

The images below show the wide variety of close-up capabilities of different cameras, lenses and accessories.

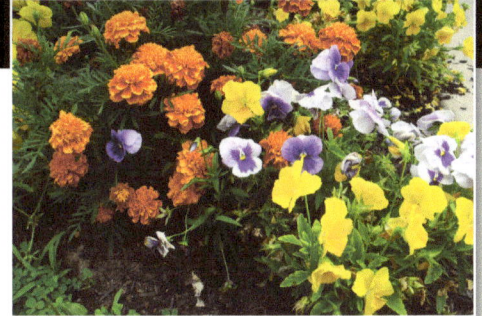

Close-focus with 18-200mm zoom set to 18mm on a DSLR.

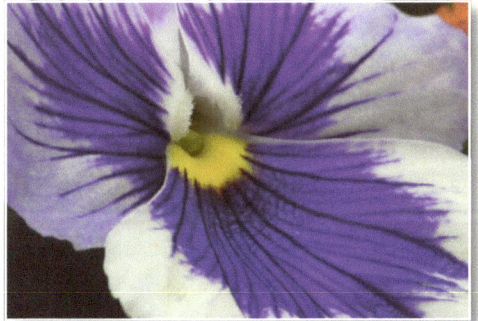

180mm Macro lens at minimum focus on a DSLR.

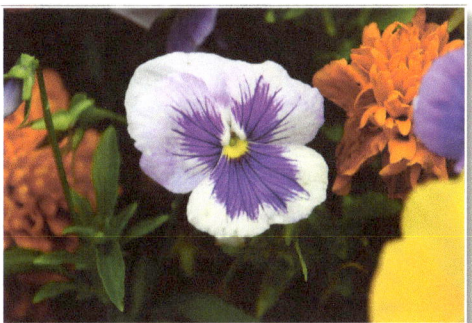

Close-focus with 18-200mm zoom set to 200mm on a DSLR.

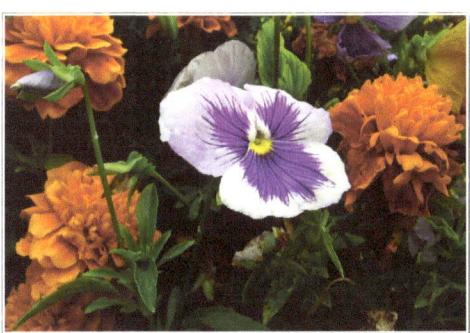

Macro setting on compact digital camera.

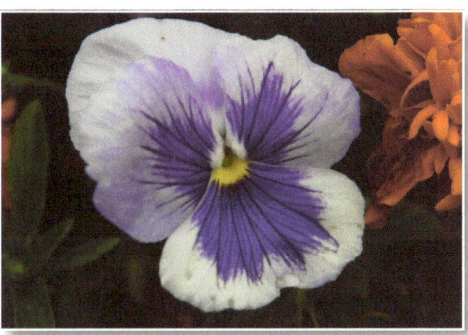

Close-focus with 18-200mm zoom set to 200mm and +1 close-up filter attached on a DSLR.

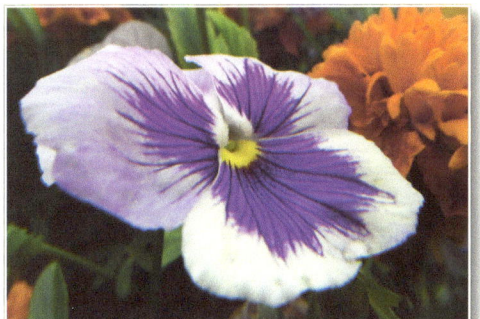

Macro setting on compact digital camera and holding a cheap $2 magnifying glass in front of the lens. Soft and distorted, it is still an acceptable image.

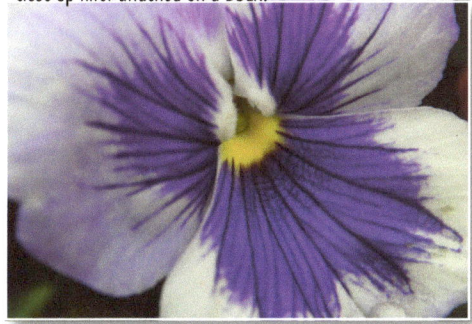

Close-focus with 18-200mm zoom set to 200mm with 25mm extension tube attached on a DSLR.

Digiscoping

Use Your Telescope

Combine your compact camera and a good quality spotting scope or telescope and you will have a lens of 3000mm or more. 3000mm is 60x magnification! Not all digitals will work well with a telescope, and not all telescopes will work well for digiscoping. A high quality scope (Leica or Swarovski are best) with a large objective (front lens) of at least 70mm will afford the best images. A digital camera with a lens diameter smaller than the scope's eyepiece diameter will work best.

The ability to center the camera's lens on the scope's eyepiece is key to quality images. The first step is to zoom the camera's lens to 3x or 4x, just enough so the circle or vignette effect is removed. Often, just holding the camera to the eyepiece of the scope will work, however, there are many adaptations that can be made to help center the camera—a whole market has sprung up specifically for digiscoping. Some adapters can be as simple as a piece of PVC tubing or as expensive as a precisely machined, threaded aluminum mount. The better designed mounts help to reduce camera shake, however, a fairly fast shutter speed is also needed to reduce subject blur.

Aim the scope and focus on the subject first, then place the camera on the eyepiece. The autofocus on the camera will "fine-tune" the focus. Exposure control is the same as when not using the scope. Remember the basics!

Though many cameras will work, the set-up shown is an older system—a Nikon Coolpix 4500 with the LensAdapter camera mount connected to a Swarovski ATS-80 HD spotting scope. This made a perfect digiscoping set-up 5 years ago, however, many newer models will work better. Models change frequently so do an on-line search to see what others are currently using. You will be amazed at how many people are digiscoping!

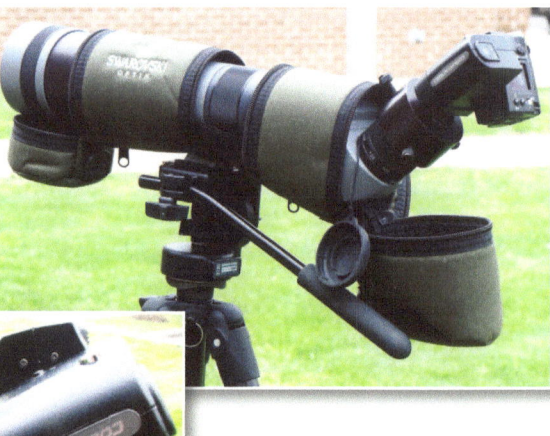

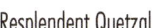

Image at left shows the full scene from the photographer's perspective. The Aplomado Falcon is in front of the two tallest palm trees ahead of the scope.

In the image below, shot with a compact digital at 200mm (35mm equivalent), the falcon is visible to the right of the flames, but not distinct. A DSLR with a bigger lens would have done better.

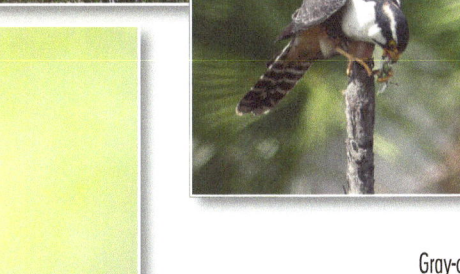

The image below was shot with the digiscoping set-up described. The 60x magnification shows all the details, even the insect the bird is eating!

Resplendent Quetzal

Gray-chested Dove

Emerald Basilisk

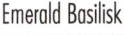

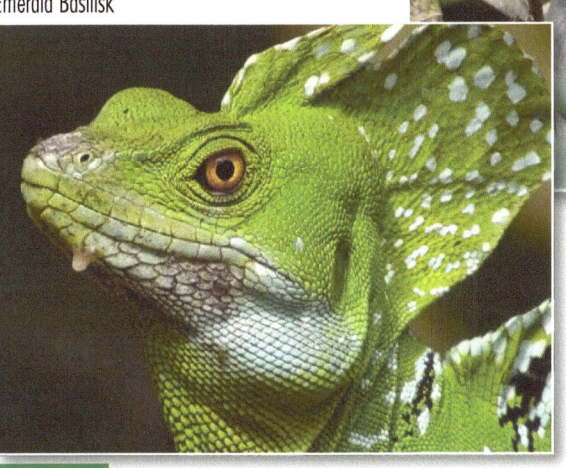

Cooperative subjects are a must with digiscoping. It is a slow form of photography, and is often best as a team of two people, but when it works the results can be amazing!

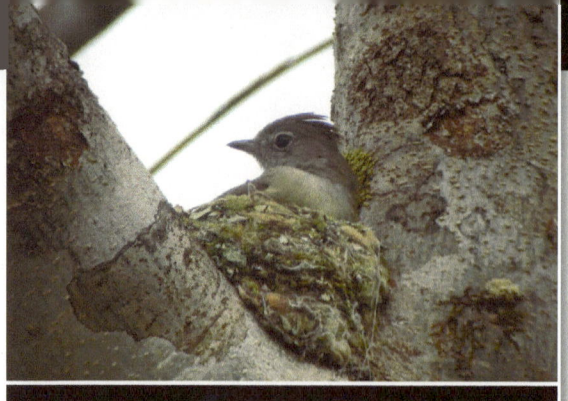

Digiscoping done right. This nesting elania is sharp and well exposed. Since the bird was not moving it was possible to capture it properly via digiscoping.

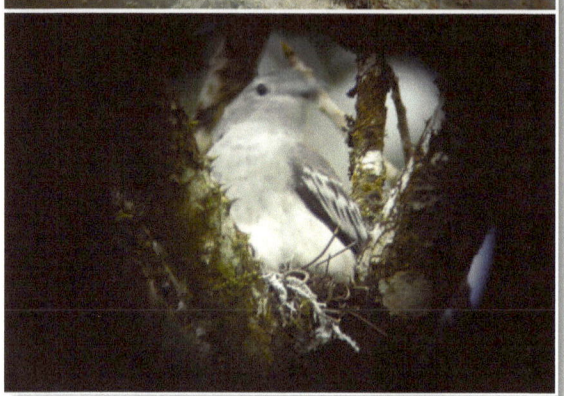

Digiscoping done wrong is bad. This nesting cotinga is almost unrecognizable because the camera was not zoomed to the proper position causing a vignette and the shutter speed was too slow.

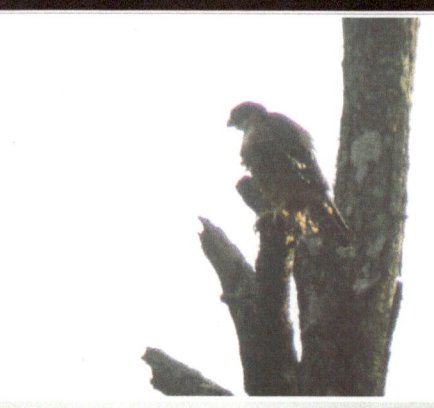

Sometimes the most important thing is to just get the shot. Proof that a particular animal was seen, such as the rarely seen Orange-breasted Falcon. Poor exposure and bad background make for a low quality, yet still recognizable image.

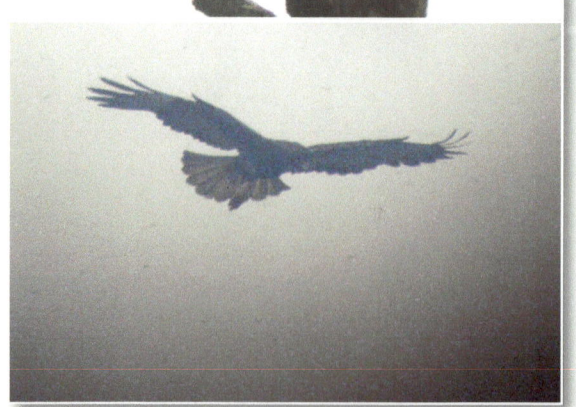

Photographing moving subjects like this White-tailed Hawk in flight is nearly impossible with digiscoping. The high magnification makes it difficult to stay with your subject.

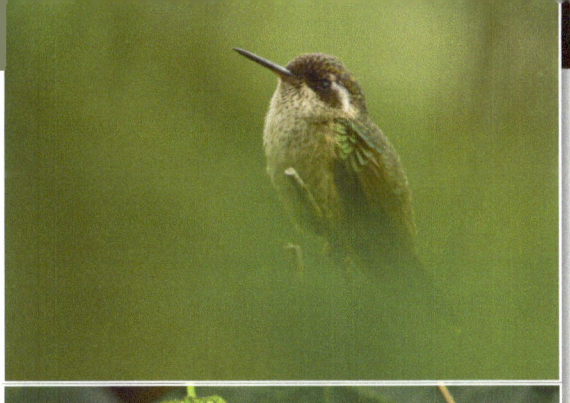

Digiscoping through leaves and branches would be difficult, however, with a DSLR's pin-point focus this Speckled Hummingbird's head is sharp, even though the body os partially obscured by leaves.

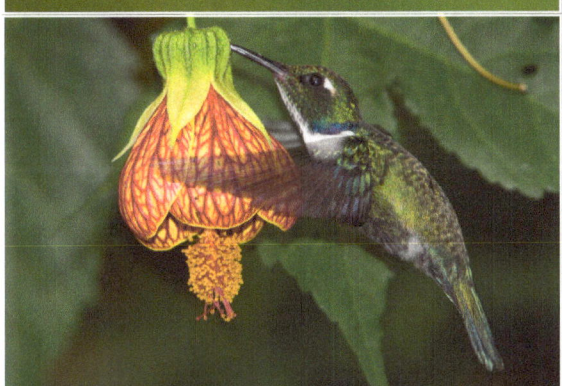

Wedge-billed Hummingbirds, like most hummingbirds, are usually moving... quickly. With a DSLR it was still difficult to track, but the image is superb.

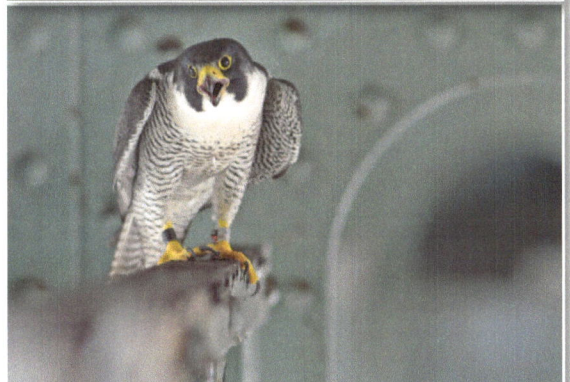

This perched Peregrine Falcon didn't stay long, but with a DSLR he was captured quick and sharp.

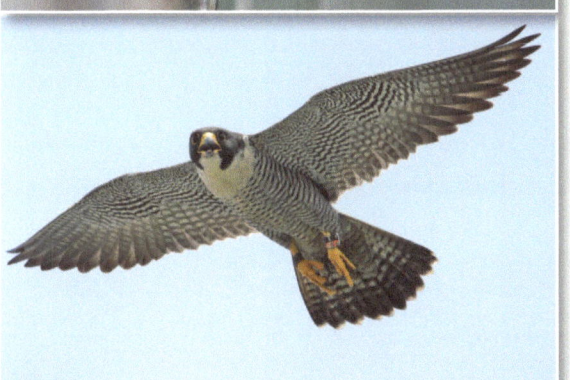

Following the fastest animal in the world is tough, getting images of this 200 MPH bird in flight is only possible with a DSLR!

Know Your Subject

Wildlife Identification

The plethora of field guides on the market today offer nature photographers no excuses for not knowing what they are photographing! Wildflowers, trees, birds, mammals, butterflies, dragonflies... anything you photograph can and should be identified. Learning more about your subjects will help you to find them easier, understand them better and create better images.

In March every year there is an amazing wildlife phenomenon in Southeast PA that few people witness. The Spotted Salamander and Wood Frog migration takes place well after dark on a rainy night when temperatures have been 40° for at least two consecutive nights is an incredible event. Several other species of salamanders may also be present... so be alert for anything that looks different!

Salamanders and frogs do not require a lot of water in which to breed. As you can see in the image above we are photographing in a trailside drainage ditch. Any vernal pool—an area that stays wet most of Spring—can be home to hundreds of salamander, frog or toad tadpoles... look, listen and observe!

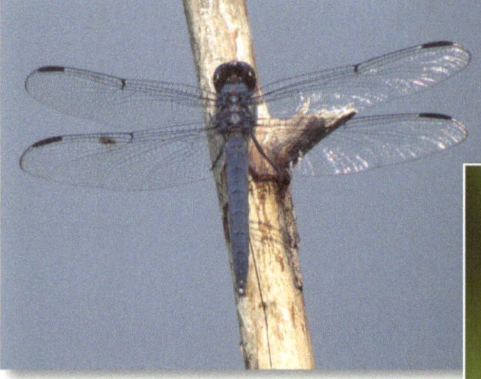

The Slaty Skimmer (left) and the Spangled Skimmer below are both "perching" dragonflies—they often come back to the same perch while hunting. These are just two of the many common dragonflies found in southeast Pennsylvania.

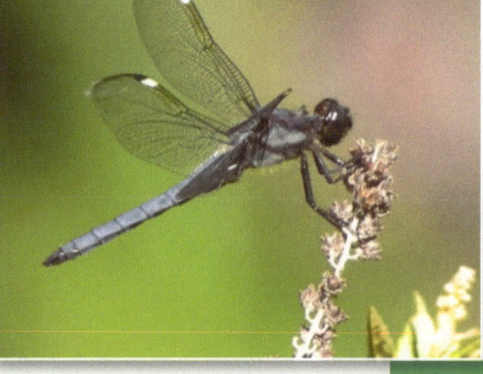

The image of the Slaty Skimmer (above) was captured with a digiscope that was pre-focused on the stick out in the marsh. Knowing that many dragonflies perch, I was prepared for its landing on the stick. In this case I did not even have to move the scope as he "composed" himself in my viewfinder!

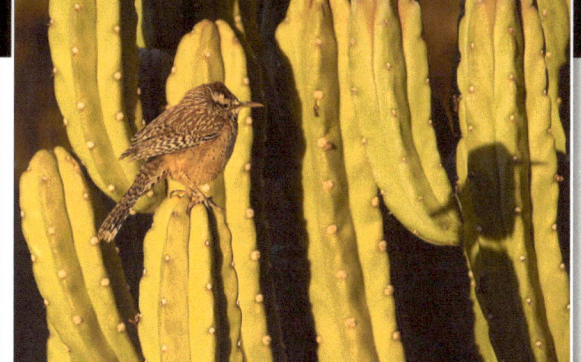

Cactus Wrens are active, especially during the prime feeding times of early morning and late evening. I observed this wren for a while, taking photos the whole time. I noticed he was heading toward the cactus which was in perfect light from the setting sun and waited for the decisive moment when I he showed me his profile that cast a recognizable shadow on the cactus.

Galapagos Marine Iguanas are very docile as well as being photogenic. Not many animals will allow you to approach this close. Be careful when approaching any wildlife, watch for signs of nervousness like head bobbing or tail flicking... that means back off!

Also, it is a good idea to know if your subject if dangerous, venomous, etc. If you are not sure, don't take a chance!

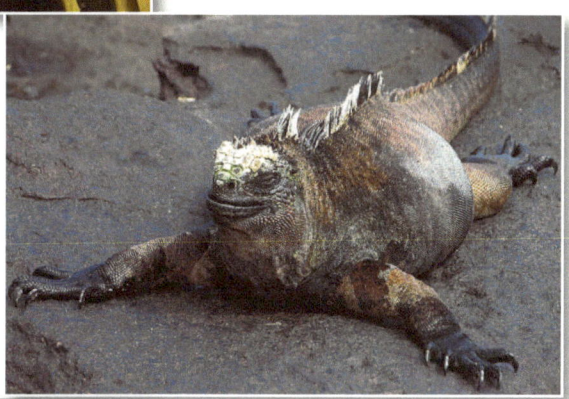

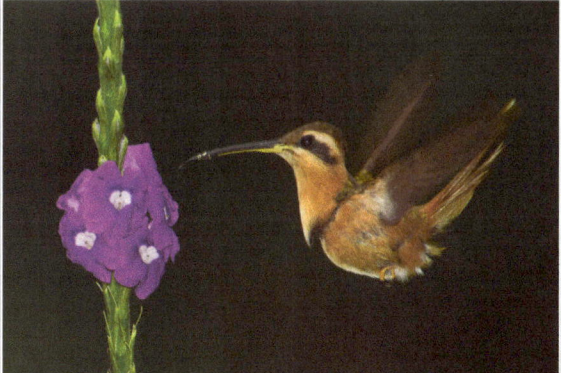

Reddish Hermits, a hummingbird species found in the Amazon Basin, are "trap-line feeders"—they follow a circuit of flowers throughout the forest. If you see them at a flower, wait about 20-45 minutes and they will be back again. Knowing the types of flowers on which they prefer to feed is helpful to catch them in action!

On a cold, dark, rainy night in March I was excited to see this Marbled Salamander, a species I had never seen before! I photographed it for quite awhile as it was very cooperative... too cooperative.

My friend had planted a plastic model when I wasn't looking. If I had learned more about this species I would have known they breed in September and would not be seen in March. She got me good and it wasn't even April 1st yet!

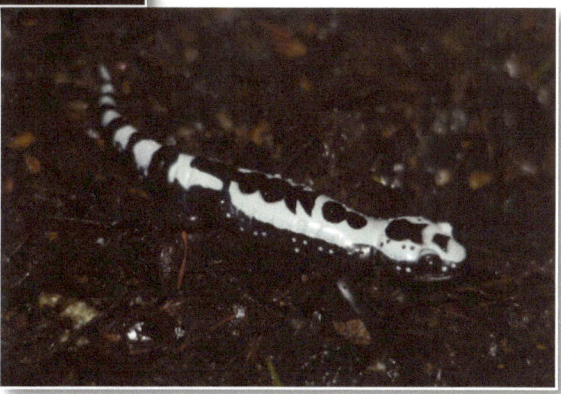

Additional Accessories

Tripod and Monopod

An obvious necessity for time-exposures, a tripod is the first step to getting the sharpest images of nature. Anytime a long telephoto lens is used a tripod will help get the best image possible. For landscape photography with a wide angle lens, a tripod helps to slow the photographer down and concentrate on composition.

A monopod is perfect for tight locations or when travelling light when just a bit more stability is needed. Because it is just a single leg, time exposures with a monopod are out of the question, however, by bracing monopod mounted camera against a tree or railing, very slow shutter speeds may be used.

UV Filter

Lens protection is the purpose of a UV filter. These clear, optical quality filters do not affect the image, but keep the lens itself from getting scratched or damaged. It is much less expensive to replace a filter than to replace a lens!

Circular Polarizing Filter

"Circular" describes the pattern in which the polarization is applied to the glass, not the shape of the filter itself! Used mainly outdoors, a polarizing filter removes glare and reflections from not only your subject, but more importantly from dust and moisture particles in the air. In doing so, the filter allows for much more color saturation and contrast in the final image. This effect is **not** something that can be done in Photoshop!

Add-on Lenses

DSLR cameras can use a wide array of interchangeable lenses, however, compacts are limited often to just the built-in zoom. Some compacts do have limited capabilities of adding a wide angle or telephoto accessory lens onto the front of the built-in lens without losing much of the quality. The built-in lens must be used at the telephoto position when adding a tele-lens and at the wide angle position if adding a wide-lens accessory, zooming with either lens cannot be done.

Image Stabilized Lenses

In recent years developments have been made that—for a price—allow photographers to hand-hold a camera at slower shutter speeds. Canon's IS lenses, Sigma's OS and Nikon's VR lenses use similar technology to reduce camera shake. Sony has a different technology that works with the image sensor in the camera to reduce shake. Many compacts use this technology as well. Remember... this reduces camera shake and not subject movement!

The Essence of Light

Look at the light

No—not at the sun... look at how the light is falling onto your subject. It is good to see what kind of light you are working with. Which way are the shadows falling? Unless you want a silhouette effect, where your subject is black against an interesting background, it's generally best to shoot with the sun behind you.

How is the light affecting your subject? Is the light blazing directly and brightly upon your whole subject? This works well if you are in love with the bold colors of your subject. Side lighting, on the other hand, can add drama but can also cause extreme, hard-to-print contrasts. Indirect light can be used to make your subject glow soft and pretty.

Weather plays a big role in nature photography. Look outside and decide whether or not you are going to want to have the sky in your picture. If it's overcast, simply keep the sky out of your pictures as much as possible. This is usually the best way to avoid both muted tones in your subject and washed-out skies in your background. However, an overcast sky is perfect for photographing flowers as the soft light casts few shadows. Overcast skies are great for photographing waterfalls as well as it will reduce the contrast of white water over dark rocks.

Sunset and sunrise will usually cast a warmer (red or yellow) glow over your subjects. This warm glow will often add a pleasing tone or mood to your image. Don't always photograph the actual sunset or sunrise, but rather look the opposite direction and find a subject within the glow of the warm light. The long shadows cast early and late in the day can often be a subject unto themselves.

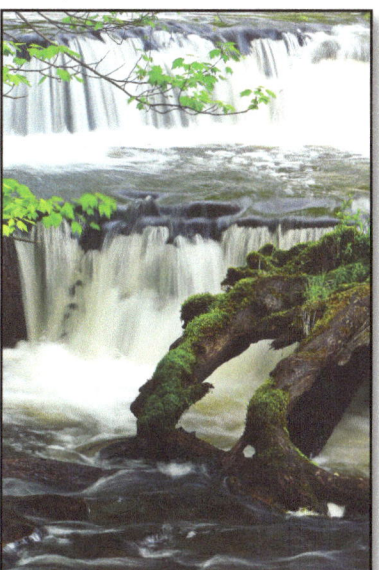 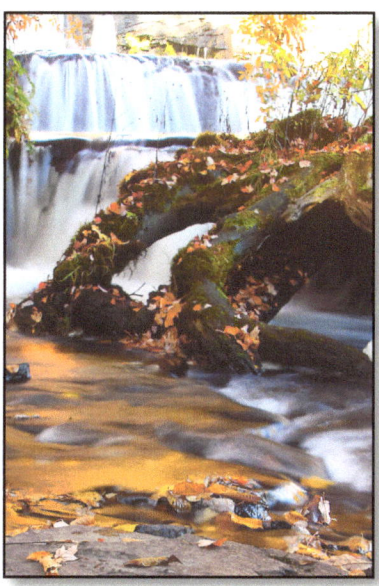

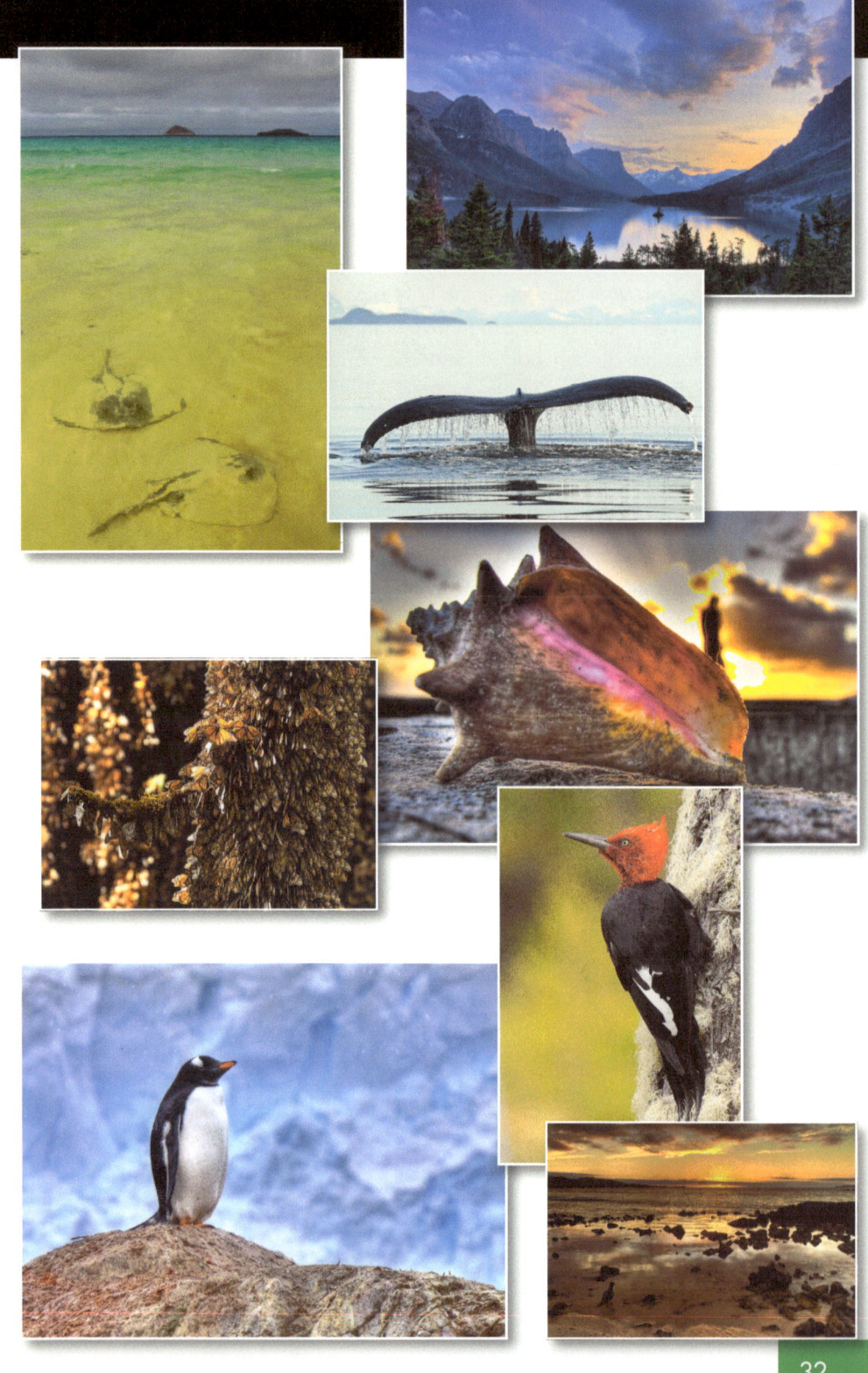

Self-Assignments

For these self-assignments, use readily available subjects such as your kids, your dog or birds on your back yard feeder. Practicing on readily available subjects will help prepare you to react quickly for those subjects that are not so common!

NOTE: Please read your instruction book thoroughly so that you understand your camera's functions, capabilities and limitations while doing these assignments!

ISO
Compare the image quality differences at different ISO settings:
• Photograph a subject at the lowest ISO on your camera
• Photograph a subject at the highest ISO on your camera

White Balance
Compare the color differences with different White Balance settings, all taken of the same subject in the same light:
• Take one photo at the Auto White Balance setting
• Take one photo on the Sunny setting
• Take one photo on the Cloudy setting

Shutter Speed
Try your hand at using shutter speeds for different effects:
• Photograph moving subject at a shutter speed of at least 1/250
• Photograph moving subject at a shutter speed of no higher than 1/30

Aperture
Notice the difference various apertures can have on your photos:
• Photograph a close-up subject at the largest aperture on your camera
• Photograph a close-up subject at the smallest aperture on your camera

Composition
Practice the rule of thirds and see the difference it can make in your photo:
• Take a landscape with the horizon in the middle of the frame
• Take the same landscape with the horizon 1/3 down from the top of the frame
• Take the same landscape with the horizon 2/3 down from the top of the frame
• Photograph a still subject centered in the frame
• Photograph the same subject using the rule of thirds and place it in the proper position in the frame.